Average Joe's Pillars of Leadership

Defining Characteristics of Leadership

Joe Hinchliffe

JoeHinchliffe.com

I0463357

Contents

Acknowledgements

The acknowledgements come at a pivotal moment for me, I write this 12 days before I fly to Australia leaving my family, friends and business behind. Out of my comfort zone and on a new journey. I realise now that I have taken my tight-knit support group for granted, believing they would always be there. And they won't. Nobody's will. Learn from me; appreciate what's right under your nose and make the most of what you have got, while it is still there.

A massive thank you to all my family, friends and readers for their support, encouragement and faith. I deeply appreciate every single one of you.

A big thank you to Emily Wilkinson for writing the foreword, a first for the Average Joe Knows Series!

Charlotte, without you this book would be grammatically incorrect and make no sense. A huge thank you for your help xxxx

AVERAGE JOE'S

Secrets to Personal Development

JOE HINCHLIFFE

FREE EBOOK – get the bestselling eBook – Average Joe's Secrets to Personal Development:

JoeHinchliffe.com

Foreword

By Emily Wilkinson

Joe is the only person I know at such a young age to have absorbed all of the dynamite knowledge he's acquired on his own journey of Personal Development and successfully conveyed it through his books in a concise and exciting manner! No matter whether you are new to Personal Development or you consider yourself to be "experienced" Joe will always offer exceptional levels of value and awareness. If you haven't yet read *"Average Joe's Secrets to Personal Development"* I'll let you in to my own secret... It's far from average!

I stumbled upon the concept of "Personal Development" when I was introduced to the Network Marketing Industry. My life changed in an instant. I was suddenly studying people that I wanted to be like. How have they got to where they are? How can I do that? I used to ask myself. I was hungry for success, but I understood I first needed to master the skills to get there.

I travelled listening to "Leaders" speak on stage, taking notes & implementing the actions I learnt into my everyday life. *"Success Rituals"* will help you do this too! Before I knew it, I myself was asked to deliver training on stage at an International Conference in Barcelona in front of 20,000 people. Talk about comfort zones, I was about to escape mine! People were asking "How have you done it?" and wanting photographs with me! Was this it? Had I become a "Leader?" I suddenly had a team and plenty of followers (a community) and soon realised for me to further develop I had to create more Leaders!

The most powerful Leadership tool you have is your own personal example. I learnt this from my Father. He went from being a one man band Joiner to being voted "Yorkshire's Business Man of the year" with 16,000 votes! He figured out his Why, had a clear vision and a bullet proof mindset (www.craigwilkinson.com). We coach Business Owner's on how to grow & improve their businesses. Our community is now huge, people travel from all over the UK to attend our monthly hybrid coaching / networking events...and more importantly they're now becoming Leader's themselves!

I would like to personally thank Joe for writing this book. It's given me even more focus and motivation. I can really identify and relate to many of the Pillars such as "Planning", "Decision" and "Integrity". If you were to implement the specific actions set out within this book I guarantee you will not only smash your goals (personal or business) but you'll successfully inspire others to do the same.

Introduction

"Become the kind of leader that people would follow voluntarily; even if you had no title or position" – Brian Tracy

Just like success, leadership is simple, but not easy. Most people have a general picture in their mind of what a leader is, for instance if I were to ask you – What is leadership? I imagine some, maybe all the following spring to mind;

- A purpose, mission, image of the future
- The strength to stand for their purpose
- Being genuine
- Thinking of others more than themselves
- Controlling their own thoughts, behaviours and actions
- An understanding of where they are going before they set off
- Painting the picture to help others see your vision for the future
- Making big choices quickly with the WHY in mind
- Hearing taking the time to understand what others have to say
- "Broad shoulders" – to carry the weight of their dream
- Ensuring others totally understand you
- Sharing knowledge

These are the 12 Pillars of Leadership

Why Do You Need To Be a Leader?

The only person who will make sure you get everything you want from life, that you die with no regrets and leave a legacy that lasts for generations, is you! It's not possible to accomplish all three and not be a leader.

Choose leadership, BUT and it's a big but, only if that is what you truly want and not because it appears that's where the glory and glamour is. The road to your success will be more than bumpy, it will be very rocky.

Why This Book?

If you're reading this you've chosen a life of leadership, and so the journey begins. But why invest your time into this book when there are 1000's of fantastic books on leadership to read?

My approach is simple, to the point and clear. I'm not one for filling sentences with words just for the sake of it or for the word count. The intention behind every sentence is to bring you value and I sincerely hope each and every one does.

I imagine life to be like a jigsaw, with everybody needing different pieces to complete their picture. This book could be the last piece to complete your picture. This excites, motivates and inspires me, and I hope it has the same effect on you.

Vision

"Create the highest and grandest vision possible for your life, because you become what you believe" – Oprah Winfrey

Successful leadership always starts with vision. What's the point in leading if we don't know why we're doing it. The reason WHY has to be huge to give us the courage to pursue a goal bigger than ourselves. Our WHY has to be big to give us the fortitude to overcome the many obstacles that'll be thrown in our path.

Vision gives us focus and direction, without it we wouldn't have a following. Who's going to follow a leader who doesn't know where they're going?

We spend time on unproductive tasks that don't move us closer to our dreams and goals. Vision provides us with clarity, so we can invest time into the 20% of tasks that are crucial and delegate the 80% of tasks that are insignificant (if you're unfamiliar with the 80/20 rule read The 80/20 Principle by Richard Koch)

Not only does vision give us meaning and purpose, it also provides us with motivation to get up and get to work. With the end result in mind, we're inspired to take action, inspired to make progress and inspired to better ourselves so we can mould the world to match the image we hold in our mind.

WHY?

Simon Sinek wrote a book on this very subject – Start With WHY – I highly recommend you read it straight after this book! In the book, Simon discusses how the majority of organisations communicate; they start with WHAT they do, then HOW they do it and finally WHY they do what they do comes last.

Great companies describe their WHY first. They tell us what they believe as they're looking for people who believe the same so they can join their community; whether as customer, employee, supplier or something else.

You cannot have vision unless you have a strong, clear and compelling WHY. A WHY is just a belief that you hold. For instance, I believe everybody has the potential to have their dream life. And by that I don't mean everybody will have the same life because we're all individuals with unique desires. But, we can have what each of us pictures the ideal life to be. For some it may be having millions in the bank, for others a new car every 5 years. Whatever it is, you can reach out and grab it if, and it's a big if, you invest in yourself, play to your strengths, develop your weakness – Grow!

If you already have your WHY, that's fantastic! Continue to go over it so it becomes more and more detailed. That way you'll be able to communicate with clarity and impact to quickly find the people with the same beliefs.

If you don't then you'll need to spend time with yourself in a quiet room, alone. This way you can really find what's at your core, with no outside influences. Your WHY will not be discovered overnight, it takes time. However, it is inside you, you just need to lure it out.

Communicate

When we're crystal clear on why we have been placed upon the earth and we have built a vison on where we are headed, we then need to communicate our vison. The purpose of telling the world is to find others who believe what we believe. No one can decide to join you if they don't know the direction you're heading in. Without others help we'll never be successful – we cannot get to the top alone.

It takes more than informing people about our vision. People don't want to be informed they want to be INSPIRED. To inspire them we are required to communicate with passion, purpose and of course – starting with our WHY! That's why it's vital to our success we believe what we speak and think.

Our actions reaffirm what we say. A leader has a responsibility to do more than they require of their followers. We must be willing to work harder, for longer than we would expect of anyone else. That doesn't mean others can take it easy; however we must set the example.

We have no choice but to be obsessed with our goal. Anything else and people will see right through as soon as we begin to convey our message.

Community

I mentioned in the last section that we cannot achieve our goal alone, we will need help along the way. Building a community of likeminded individuals around our vision who all believe in the change we are creating is essential.

Whether your community is a business, charity or sports team it will need a shared purpose to bring everyone together. Ensuring every member knows what they are working towards is essential. What's even more important is helping people take your vision and make it their own. Members of the group will need a sense of ownership if they are to stay committed to the cause. It's easy keeping people when times are good, it's when times are challenging that our faith is tested. If the community fully believes in the vision, they will give it everything to make it a reality.

As a leader you are there to serve your community. You can do this by finding out what's important to them. As much as you will be passionate about how you can make your vision happen and want to share your ideas, it's critical you listen to them. Give them time to contribute. Actually listen, acknowledge what's been said. If there's any great ideas – journal and act on them.

Big Picture

As the community grows it's easy to get lost in small day to day decisions, things that don't move us closer to the picture we hold in our mind. Aside from the community, life will throw things at us that we cannot cast aside. Life and the community don't have an off switch to let us work tirelessly towards our goal.

It can be frustrating putting our dream to one side so we can work on the 'small stuff', but keeping perspective helps. Keep in mind success isn't achieved over night, despite what the media would have us believe. And if we've discovered our WHY, we'll keep working no matter how long it takes. The small stuff may get in the way from time to time, but we'll always come back to our mission.

Taking the long view doesn't mean giving up on our hopes and dreams. Nor does it mean waiting and complaining until we realise our dream. It means doing what we can right now, with what we have – being patient, but focused.

Goals

Having the bigger picture in mind is effective when making day to day decisions. The only downside is the dream can seem far away. This is where short term goals help. Having a smaller target to aim for that keeps us in line with our vision provides extra motivation.

The key is ensuring the goals match our WHY. If they don't, they're distractions. One way to do this is to start at our

WHY and work our way back to where we are now. For instance, let's say your WHY is to fully fund 1000 children's education in Africa and to do that you'll need $1,000,000. Before you earn $1 million, you'll need to learn how to make $500,000, $250,000 etc. So your first goal may be to learn how to make $50,000. Once this is achieved you'll keep changing the target until you acquire what you need to accomplish the vision.

Not only is goal setting valuable for personal use, leaders can set goals for the individuals of the community. This isn't setting the goals for the team members, rather asking the right questions so they can set their own goals. Some example questions are;

- What drives you?
- What would you hope people would say at your funeral?
- If we could jump 5 years' head, what would you hope your life would be like?

From this goals we can help team members build their own vision.

Courage

*"Courage doesn't always roar.
Sometimes courage is the quiet voice at
the end of the day saying, 'I will try
again tomorrow' "– Mary Anne
Radmacher*

A key characteristic for successful leadership. It takes courage to not only stand for something, but to go one step further and pursue your vision, your WHY. To say to anybody who will listen, this is what I believe, this is what I want to achieve, this is how I will shape the world.

At the time of writing this book, if you Google – 'define courage', it produces two responses;

1) the ability to do something that frightens one; bravery.
2) strength in the face of pain or grief.

Many of us believe that to be brave or courageous we must not experience fear when in reality the opposite is true. Instead, we must Feel The Fear and Do It Anyway. If you haven't read the book with the same title, it's a must to add to your library. Pushing through the fear and taking the actions that are required of us is the only known way to avoid one of the worst feelings a human can experience – regret.

There's a superb quote from E. E. Cummings – "It takes courage to grow up and be who you really are". Bear in mind this was said over 50 years ago, I believe it to be more significant now and will continue to be more relevant as time goes on; the reason being the pressure on us to fit into society grow day by day.

Risks

Being the leader of any community forces us to have the courage to take risk with no assurance of success. There are no guarantees, it could all end in failure.

If we have the choice between two products and we can only support one, we as the leader, have to decide. Yes, we can gather detailed product, market and consumer information, but ultimately the buck stops with us. Often the risk forces us out of our comfort zone and into the unknown.

To get past the fear of failure it helps to change our attitude towards it. Failure is normally viewed as bad, something to be avoided at all costs. However, if we view failure as an opportunity to grow, either as an individual or a community, the thought of not getting our desired result doesn't seem as scary. As long as the same errors are not being made time and time again, failure can be a massive learning opportunity.

Only you can decide what you are prepared to risk, some may risk the future of the community with one decision, others only risk 1% or less. If we take risks with our WHY and vision in mind we will achieve our dream.

Say What Needs To Be Said

It's uncomfortable. It's awkward. It's crucial. A courageous conversation is needed. We've all been there, feeling overworked and underpaid or wanting to give feedback to a colleague but are afraid we'll cause offence. We take a deep breath, hopefully not our last, and the words grudgingly leave our mouth.

Difficult conversations take skill, practice and a sincere desire to do good. Our ability to speak up and voice our opinion is vital to our success not only in business, but in life. If you've had trouble in the past hopefully these tips will help.

Just like our WHY, we have to mean what we say. People will see straight through us if we're just saying something to 'score points'. Be genuine and your community will know you only have their best interests at heart.

There are always two sides to every story. Before we dive into the situation be sure to get all the information so we can state the facts clearly. As much as 'he said, she said' is entertaining on soap operas, it's unlikely to be beneficial to the community and the vision.

Remember that everyone is just doing their best at this moment in time. If people are being aggressive or hostile, there may be other issues at hand. Whatever comes up, you will handle it.

Follow Your Gut

I am a natural over thinker. If you're one too you'll know what it's like when a challenge comes our way. For those that don't know, it's a constant stream of thoughts on the different possibilities that may or may not arise. Over thinkers are logical people, that's why we over think. Making decisions based on logic, rather than because it feels right, results in many variables being considered.

It takes courage to make a decision because it feels right, especially when logically a different choice is more favourable. Sometimes it has to be done, we have to go with our gut.

I faced the same dilemma when I left my 'safe' accounting job to join my Dad's Window Cleaning Franchise. Logically, I was better staying, as to work with my Dad I'd be taking home a third of the salary (this continued for 18 months!) and working 50% extra hours. However, I just couldn't shake the feeling that if I didn't take the opportunity I would regret it.

Thankfully, I worked with my Dad and everything, eventually, worked out better than I imagined. In fact, without taking my guts advice I wouldn't be where I am today.

Face Fears

Many fears have to be faced when leading a team. This becomes more apparent as the community grows. We go from having a raw idea to someone who is looked upon to motivate, inspire and guide the community to the finish line.

As a result, there are 5 major fears the majority of leaders need to push past;

Criticism. Our shortcomings will be mentioned more than our victories. A leader should expect criticism, it's something you'll have to get used to. Feedback and criticism should be taken seriously, but not to heart. If you believe it to be valid, learn and grow from it. Otherwise don't give it another thought.

Failure. There's no getting away from it. Failing at anything hurts. And so it should; I hope it hurts so much it's makes you never want to experience it again. Our mistakes are there to learn from so we never repeat again.

Making Decisions. As a leader your community will look to you when a decision needs making. Vision and courage will come into play when deciding which route to choose. Making decisions is not about selecting the correct choice, but rather being certain you have. You may be wrong however be certain in your wrongness.

Speaking. The fear of public speaking is one of the most common fears worldwide, some people fear it more than death! Overcoming the fear is all down to practice and confidence. The more you practice, the more confident you become. Start with a small group and when it becomes comfortable increase the size.

Responsibility. If you're a Spiderman fan you'll know that with great power comes great responsibility. Not only are you responsible for the success of the vision, there's also the customers, employees and suppliers to name a few. This can weigh heavy on a leader's shoulders, that's the reason your WHY has to be huge. Also keep in mind that all anyone can ask of you is for you to give your best effort.

Persevere

Life is going to go against you at some point. Challenges, obstacles and setbacks are going to come your way. There is no running or hiding, they will find you. How they're handled will have a massive impact on your success.

So why persevere if it's impossible to avoid the road blocks on route to your success? If you don't know the answer to this question, your WHY isn't huge enough. And that's okay. It's better to find out early rather than after you have invested time, money and energy.

When your WHY is big enough for you to want to overcome any challenge you are presented with, the next question is, how do you overcome them? I can't give specific solutions, nor are there any books on resilience. The best piece of advice I can give you comes from the time I met Napoleon Hill's Grandson – J. B. Hill. His words of wisdom we're "Grow yourself bigger than the challenges you face".

Growth is the only way to overcome the roadblocks in your way. Be better today than you were yesterday.

Integrity

"The true measure of a man is how he treats someone who can do him absolutely no good" – Samuel Johnson

When no one is watching do you still behave the same? It's easier to act a certain way when people are watching, but when no one's there, that's when our true colours show. An individual of integrity will be the same no matter who's around, be that the President of the United States, their friends or nobody.

Integrity requires an element of courage. To speak up and say what we really think takes guts, more so when our point of view goes against the majority. It is so much easier to conform to society or the community, than to be yourself and state your opinion.

Leaders speak the truth, even when it hurts. At the core of integrity is truthfulness. Individuals will not follow a leader who isn't completely honest. Being honest from the start will attract other honest individuals (like attracts like, the Law of Attraction) and create a culture of truthfulness.

An often overlooked side to integrity is work ethic. Coming in early and staying late to get things done for the community is an example all leaders will hope to set. Our actions speak louder than words. Not only must we talk the talk, it's vital we walk the talk too.

Honesty

Integrity and honesty go hand in hand. In the intro to this chapter I briefly touched on truthfulness, now we'll delve a little deeper.

Why be honest? It's a question you will have asked at some point, simply because it can be hard. It's easy to be honest when we agree, however when we disagree it's another matter entirely. We should be honest because we want people to be honest with us, even when the truth hurts.

In times gone by, leaders were believed to be honest because of their position, now the opposite is more likely to be true. When we see someone of authority we assume they're dishonest, it's human nature – "Who did they have to step on to get that job" – we've all thought it at one time. Now leaders have to prove they're honest. A fantastic opportunity to do that is when we make a mistake.

Admitting we're wrong shows we are truthful - why would we lie about being wrong? Members of your community will develop trust for the person who displays honesty. Trust doesn't appear overnight, but it can grow with a consistent showing of integrity, honesty and accountability.

Authentic

Authenticity is about being honest with yourself. If we are authentic, everything we say and do we actually believe. We don't just say things because they look good or because that's what we think people want to hear. We speak about what we believe. Whether it be right or wrong, good or bad, it's what we believe.

If we don't speak what we believe our community will see right through us. Even if our leadership and instructions are productive, people will be uncomfortable following a leader who doesn't mean what they say. And it doesn't just affect the group, there's the effect it has on you. Having to be a different person day after day, year after year, will wear you down until you can no longer keep up the facade.

To be authentic you'll need the courage to be yourself and the vison to put the community's goals ahead of your own self-interest. Another key ingredient is self-awareness. To be aware of your strengths, limitations and emotions is not only pivotal to being genuine, it's critical for success in any calling. Being self-aware is a journey, one which you will complete.

Example

When leaders show the way with the right actions, the community copies them and succeeds. It's that simple. You can tell them how to behave and what to do or, you can show them. Leaders cannot expect their followers to be courageous, behave with integrity, act responsible and not display the same characteristics. The tribe would look for another leader.

Take Martin Luther King Jr for example, did he know his WHY? Rather than give his "I have a plan" speech, King gave his famous "I have a Dream" speech. 250,000 people showed up to witness it, and every single one knew why they were there. They knew because Martin knew and he communicated it. If King hadn't showed what he believed very few people, if any, would have turned up. He lead by example.

Mahatma Gandhi is another leader who shows the way. Before Gandhi began leading the people, they used violence as the method to achieve their goals. For years' riots had been common against the British establishment. However, Gandhi's vision was for a nonviolent civil disobedience and non-cooperation. Despite the British massacring one thousand people in 1919, Gandhi asked for the people to not fight back. And they did as was asked because Gandhi set the example. His community watched what their leader did and mirrored him.

Keep Your Word

"My word is my bond" is how the old saying goes. If you say you're going to do something make sure you do it. Your community needs a leader they can count on, one that will deliver exactly when they said they would. Keeping your word is the essence of integrity.

As a leader you must honour your commitments even when it is difficult, expensive or inconvenient. Failing to do so risks losing the relationship equity that could have taken years to build. Not only that, when the community hear about it, they will lose respect and trust. If this happens frequently, over a period of time the tribe will feel they cannot depend on you. Leaving them no choice but to find a new, more honourable leader.

Keeping your word is not the easiest thing. Many people may want a chunk of what you offer so that you may become stretched with your time. One way to combat this is being aware of how much time you have to give out. If you don't have the time to help, say NO! It is better to say no than having the community depending on you when you can't deliver.

Personal Growth

The word "integrity" is from the Latin adjective integer (whole, complete). Integrity would then mean a sense of wholeness, from being honest, truthful and true to oneself pointing towards a consistency of character. How do we become more consistent of character? We grow!

Personal growth is of paramount importance. I believe it to be the number one fundamental that holds the majority of us back from achieving our dreams. This is the reason I wrote my first book on the subject – Average Joe's Secrets to Personal Development. If we grow our character bigger than our goals, what stops us from realising them? Nothing!

The ONLY thing preventing you from having what you desire is You!

The bucks stops with you. We cannot change the cards we have been dealt- where we grew up, what our parents did for a career, where we went to school. However, we can do our best with what we have. We can invest in ourselves, improve our weaknesses and amplify our strengths.

A good question to ask is "who do I have to become to achieve my goal?". Once you've answered that, another great question is; "Who am I right now?". From those two questions you have an ending and a beginning, all that's left is the journey.

Humility

The most undervalued trait in a leader. Our natural reaction is humility and leadership cannot go together, they are oil and water! Humility brings images of an individual who lacks confidence, is weak and uncertain, generally a pushover. If a leader displays any of these qualities, they won't be a leader for very long.

When we think of leadership the first attributes that spring to mind are strength, charisma, an expert problem solver, has all the answers, someone who runs into the blazing battlefield and carries out the wounded soldiers.

On first glance, it would appear that a humble leader is unsuccessful. However, when we recognise that a leader's job is to serve the community, a shift in perspective occurs. If we ask the question "How can a leader serve their community?" humility appears at the centre.

Humility is having a low view of our own importance – we are a small cog within the bigger picture. As leaders we must meet the needs of our tribe, know that we don't have all the answers and appreciate that we can and will make mistakes. We are not a big deal. Our community, it's purpose and the people who join you, are the big deal.

Value Others

Every single person on the planet is unique. There are no two people the same, we all have different strengths, dreams, characteristics, interests, perspectives, backgrounds. The world would be a boring place if nobody was different.

Every person you meet will be able to do at least one thing better than you. Therefore, we can learn at least one thing from everybody. If you think of how many people you interact with per week, I imagine it's a minimum of 100 (that's only 15 people a day!). Now imagine you learn 1 thing from everybody, over the course of a year that's 5200 new skills, ideas and thoughts flowing through your mind. Who is more likely to achieve their goals; the person with or the person without 5200 new pieces of knowledge?

The only way you will extract the golden nuggets is by valuing people. By taking the time to understand what they have to offer. Hear them. Actually listen to them. Appreciate them. When you think about the probability of them being born, it's a miracle that they are here, interacting with you. Remember this the next time you're in a hurry and someone wants a moment of your time.

You May Be Wrong

Most of us will do anything to avoid being wrong. We like being right. It starts when we are at school, being praised for the correct answer by the teacher and being laughed at by our peers for the wrong one. This stretches into adult life where we avoid failure like the plague.

Yet it's a fact of life; we are going to make mistakes. Some of them will be small, spilling milk or forgetting to call a client, others will be huge, investing in the wrong business or trying to do everything yourself. Winston Churchill said it best "Success is stumbling from failure to failure with no loss of enthusiasm. "

Failing and making mistakes gives us a fantastic opportunity to gain the respect from our followers. We must fight against the fear of our peers laughing and admit to being wrong. People don't expect perfection, what they want is an honest leader who they can trust. Be the example and admit to your mistakes, this will make your followers feel safe resulting in them announcing theirs. When the team can share mistakes openly, less accusations are thrown around and more responsibility is taken.

Answers

Everyone is looking for them. The community has a lot of questions and expects you to have all the answers. But you don't and this causes some hair pulling moments. Before you lose all your hair, let me reassure you; it is impossible for you to have all the answers. It will never happen. And if you believe you have them all, you're deluded and probably don't listen to your tribe.

For the realistic readers who remain; Simon Sinek says it perfectly "The role of a leader is not to come up with all the great ideas, but to encourage an environment in which great ideas can happen". And if we combine this with Napoleon Hill's mastermind principle "The mastermind principle consists of an alliance of two or more minds working in perfect harmony for the attainment of a common definite objective. Success does not come without the cooperation of others" it becomes obvious that the key to finding solutions is bringing people together who share the same dream.

The next time you are faced with an unanswered question, collect key members of your team and put the question to the group. Community enhancing ideas are sure to flow.

Value All Ideas

Now you have ideas whizzing past you left, right and centre it's extremely important to listen to every single one – even the strange ones. Here's why; if your team feel they are not being heard they will stop sharing their thoughts. When that happens you are on your own, back to pulling your hair out with the responsibility of finding answers.

Every idea should be appreciated and valued as you never know which ones might take off. Take the ice cream cone as an example; ice cream was served in dishes until 1904 when a stall at a fair ran out of plates. The adjacent Persian waffle stall had hardly sold anything. The two owners had the idea to roll the waffles and put the ice cream on top - the world has never been the same since!

A member of your community may suggest something that appears crazy which may lead to you stumbling upon the next 'ice cream cone'. Or it may just be a bonkers idea. Either way ideas and creativity are flowing; Success is sure to follow.

Gratitude

Gratitude is a powerful behaviour which can revolutionize your leadership. It demands a response, and that response is habitually positive. A natural reaction is gaining respect and trust from the community. Throughout the book I've discussed the value of the tribe trusting and respecting their leader.

A genuine display of gratitude is a near guaranteed way to build both; with genuine being the key word. If you are not truly grateful most people, especially those with a high degree of emotional intelligence will see right through you and it will have the opposite effect – a loss of respect and trust.

Being specific in your recognition washes away doubt as to whether your gratitude is legitimate. Rather than telling a team member they do a great job it is more significant to provide detail. For instance, you could tell them "Since you joined, we haven't a single complaint about our service. You're fantastic and I'm really grateful you are part of this team."

Not only does this inspire trust and respect, it also motivates your team to take action. Showing you are grateful for the work they do encourages them to put in more effort. When the team is rewarded for their effort in such a way, they are encouraged to put in more blood, sweat and tears.

Self-Discipline

"By constant self-discipline and self-control you can develop greatness of character" – Grenville Kleiser

You may be wondering why self-discipline is important in leadership – I mean isn't it all about the community? And it absolutely is, that's why you need to set the example. I've already talked about Martin Luther King and Mahatma Gandhi being examples to their tribe and the importance of that.

It is vital you set the example of self-discipline more than any other leadership pillar. Simply put, if you cannot control yourself you will never control others. It is true to say that some members of the community will follow you even if you lack self-discipline. However, the intelligent followers, the ones who have the potential and the desire to lead will not. They will go in search of another leader.

Anybody can put in the work when they feel like it, they are in a great mood and having a good day. It is when the chips are down and the mood is low that really marks the difference between a leader who changes the world and one who is changed by the world.

When it comes to leadership, I would define self-discipline as the ability to carry out the work even when we don't feel like it. That is a lot easier said than done.

Thoughts

"We become what we think about". One of the most famous phrases in the personal development field. Earl Nightingale spoke these words back in 1956 in his motivational speech, The Strangest Secret, they are still as true today as they were back then.

Before we can control what we do we must control our thoughts. Every action once started out as a thought, we have to think about doing something before we actually do. Now I appreciate that sounds incredibly obvious but this is where self-discipline begins – in the mind.

At one time you have probably had an inner battle, you know you need to do something but it's easier to not do it or to do something else, take dieting as an example. You want to lose weight so you started this brand new, 21st century diet. Some point during your new health kick it's easier to have fast food or you have an incredibly strong urge for your favourite candy bar. An inner debate entails between keeping on track with the diet and treating yourself to fast food. A self-disciplined leader stays on the diet, not deviating from the plan.

The same is true for your vision. There's work to be done but you want to have fun, take a break or just go home. The key to overcoming the undisciplined thoughts is remembering WHY you started. Remember WHY you want to lose weight, remember WHY you started the tribe, remember your vision.

Focus

Do one thing at once. This is definitely something I struggle with. When a brilliant opportunity comes my way I find it hard to resist, I like to go all in. There was a time when I was heavily involved in the day to day running of four businesses. It didn't last more than a few months because I couldn't give each community my full focus.

Great ideas come when we can immerse ourselves completely, in one vision. To do that we need the self-control to say no to both the good and the bad opportunities that come our way. Now the bad ones are easy to brush aside, it's the good ones that make you feel you have thrown a winning lottery ticket away.

Not only is it focusing on one vision that determines our success as a leader, but focusing on one task too. When working on a task it's easy to want to move on before completing it because you have so much to do. However, that task isn't going to complete itself, it'll still be unfinished when you come back to it. It is much better to finish one task then move onto the next so your mind can generate ideas solely on one thing.

Simple Rules

Are you feeling uncomfortable? Rules do that to me too! It may be better to think of the following as guidelines.

Whatever you call them, the idea is to set some conditions which you will commit to regardless of how you feel, what your friends are doing or what's on Netflix's. There is no compromising despite what's going on around, they must be upheld.

Some example 'rules' are;

Waking at 6am

Don't let anybody tell you there aren't enough hours in the day. Find those hidden hours and use them to work on building the vision.

Read for 30 Minutes Daily

All leaders are readers. Leaders devour books like they are going out of fashion. Investing in yourself with personal development is a great way to stay ahead of the field.

Exercise 4 Times a Week

Regular exercise will help release stress and tension which builds up from your hard work. Clearing both the mind and body so you are rejuvenated to take on the next day.

Carrying out the rules regularly makes them easier to form habits, and once that happens they will feel like natural parts of your life. You will start doing them without thinking.

Beat Procrastination

The silent killer of dreams – procrastination. I call it this because when you put something off, in the moment, it doesn't seem that important. At the end of the day if you've let a few tasks fall by the wayside it doesn't seem like such a bad day. However, enough of those days added up will lead to unproductive year and ultimately, an unproductive life.

Procrastination is natural, it's our inability to come to terms with this and combat it that sends us floating through life not making any progress. The strange thing about the silent killer of dreams is it's a self-imposed limitation. It all goes on in our head. There are no lack of resources such as money, equipment, or time which stop us from working. In fact, I find the more time I have, the more I procrastinate. I believe this to be because I know I can complete the task and so can 'waste time'.

If you too are like me and procrastinate when you have more time, I offer this solution. Set each task a time limit and write it on your to-do list. This way you will have created a sense of urgency and are more likely to complete your objectives.

Reward

Why do we miss out on the foods we love; to lose weight? Why do we sleep less so we can work long hours; to realise our vision? Why do we refrain from watching too much TV; to be productive?

All three questions have the same thing in common, there's a sacrifice – we give something up – and eventually, a reward. There would be no discipline without a reward. Why would we give something up that provides us with immediate gratification and sometimes, replace it with a laborious task when there is no reward at the end? We wouldn't. The reward is our motivation. It's the thing that drives us, it's that little voice in our head that keeps us disciplined when it would require less effort to stop, it is ultimately, our WHY.

However, our WHY can take a long time to realise, months, maybe years and possibly decades. It can be difficult to stay disciplined, to keep sacrificing when the reward seems so far away. Which provokes the questions why wait to reward yourself?

You don't have to wait until the end of the project to reward yourself. Set milestones along the way which when achieved you reward yourself. The reward could be a 'cheat meal' or a movie, anything you would enjoy.

What's more you can use this as a carrot and stick. If you're struggling to complete a small task, say to yourself that if you work 1 hour, without distractions, you will reward yourself with something you want to be rewarded with.

Planning

"Planning is bringing the future into the present so you can do something about it now" – Alan Lakein

Some of the greatest minds, most notably Benjamin Franklin and Napoleon Hill in his bestselling book, Think and Grow Rich, have said "If you fail to plan, you are planning to fail".

In fact, Napoleon Hill goes into more detail; "Successful leaders must plan their work and work their plan. Leaders who move by guesswork, without practical, definite plans are comparable to a ship without a rudder. Sooner or later they will land on the rocks".

I'm not going to lie to you, planning is not the most interesting aspect of leadership. Vision and courage are far more appealing, however it is essential. First, we must know where we are going and then we need to know how to get there – planning is the how.

Take going on a journey from London to Sydney as an example. If we were to set off without knowing where the airport is, we wouldn't be leaving the country. And if the pilot hasn't already planned the route it is very likely we would not land in Australia, let alone Sydney. The direction the plane is headed must be exact, if it is more than a few degrees out the destination will be hundreds of miles off course due to the distance being travelled. Preparation is key. If we are to succeed, it is imperative we plan to win.

Reverse Engineer

This simply means, start at the end and work backwords to where you currently are. You plot how to get to where you want to be. As I mentioned earlier the first step is knowing where you are going – the vision. When you have the vision ask "In a perfect world what would you want to happen in 10 years?" Now work backwards!

It isn't something to be done once, put on your wall and looked at occasionally. It is a constant process, it's a habit that needs exercising every day. Effort and focus are required to have your mind on the finish in everything you do.

This is something VaynerMedia cofounder and CEO, Gary Vaynerchuk is exceptional at. Being a regular watcher of his YouTube shows it is plain to see his end game is; "if I am 80 years old and still a business man, how do I want to be talked about?" He talks about this a lot!

I appreciate this advice isn't as practical as someone saying get out of bed at 6am or finish the most important tasks first. But, keeping the finish line at the forefront of your mind ensures what you are doing is right for you.

Be a Planner

"Don't start the day until you have it finished on paper first" – Jim Rohn

Do you run the day, or does the day run you? If you start work without knowing exactly what you are going to do, the day runs you. Take any successful person and ask them what they are going to accomplish today – all of them will be able to tell you. Not one will say "I don't know!"

You are probably wondering "if it's that simple why doesn't everybody do it?" – Because it's hard. It takes more effort, thought and discipline to plan every day than it does to just turn up and work on whatever you feel like. However, if your WHY is big and vision clear, planning your day is inescapable.

If you have read my previous books, you'll know I like to keep it simple and how I plan my day is just the same. Before I go to sleep, I write in my pocket journal tomorrow's date, underline it and then put all the task I want to complete below.

The first ones are the tasks I do every day without fail such as writing this book, the gym, reading and journaling. After that comes one off tasks, letters to customers, creating a new email for my readers and attending a client meeting. And finally, next to each task I write how much time I want to invest on it. The aim is always to finish sooner and beat the time!

Once the task is completed you get the joyous feeling of crossing it off the list! There's more information on planning the day and journaling in Secrets to Personal Development.

3 Questions

There are three questions I ask when planning; these apply to working out, writing this book and everything in between.

The first is "What do I want?" And it's not as straightforward as "a car" or "$1 million", you need to be as clear and specific as possible. If you want a car state the make, model, price, colour, leather seats, blue steering wheel. Details matter. Write them down. Thoughts become things when they are placed on paper.

Question number two is "Why?" What is your reason for wanting the above? I've talked about your WHY throughout this book and your reason for desiring the car may be your WHY, however it may be more specific too. Make sure your clearly define it and jot that down too!

The third question – "How are you going to get there?" This is the least important question mainly because what determines whether you reach the result is 80% why and only 20% how. If your reason is strong the how will fall into place.

The last bit is not, so much a question just something to keep in mind, focus on the result not activities. If your aim is to get a response from a client, don't focus on the number of emails sent or calls made. The goal is a response, not the amount of voicemails you left!

Adapt

Now you have invested hours in planning your vision and goals I'm going to give you some gut-wrenching news – your plan will change. Nothing ever goes to plan. But, I can hear you screaming "my plan is so refined it considers time for errors! "

Even the best of plans will need adjustment. Yes, you may have taken into account the worst-case scenario, and have another plan for the best. Be that as it may, life will throw you a curve ball, the next Facebook may launch or there may be another recession or a family member may move to another country.

How you view change will determine your success. If the overriding thought is to give up as the vision isn't sticking to plan, you will fail. On the other hand, if your mindset is, how can I use this knew situation to my advantage – you are ready to succeed. The obstacles of life are intended to make us better! Use them. Learn from them! Be better!

If you're looking for extra study on dealing with change check out Who Moved My Cheese by Spencer Johnson.

Implement

The plan is all set, you're ready; Is the community ready? The first step in implementation is getting the team fully behind the idea. Just like the vision, one of the keys to getting their backing is how you communicate. Be clear, be passionate and show how it relates to your common purpose – the community's WHY. Paint the picture in their minds of not only why we need to do this, but how this plan will take us there.

Planning is a process not an event. Creating the plan is a starting point, keeping the plan as a visible reference point is more important. As leaders, we must be held accountable if the targets set out in the plan are not hit or exceeded. The first piece of the vision to hold you accountable needs to be you. If you are not achieving the results don't be deluded, be honest. Then you can focus on why this is the case and how you can improve.

The community is the second element of the vision which must hold you accountable. They will know if you are the reason the plan is not working and for the good of the vision, plus to help you grow as a person and a leader, they have to express their concerns.

Influence

"Influence is our inner ability to lift people up to our perspectives" – Joseph Wang

You can influence without being a leader but, there can be no leadership without influence. Influence is a person's ability to shape people and mould outcomes.

This is how leaders lead. On one level, it's about compliance, getting a person to go along with what you believe. Peer pressure is a great example of this! But you need more of a genuine commitment to accomplish big tasks and goals than you do to bunk off school.

Make no mistake about it, you need the right people on the bus and the right people in the community around you for influence to be effective. If you hire a red wine enthusiast at a white wine company, it's highly unlikely you are going to affect their decision making.

Affecting key decisions is why we need influence. As a leader, we have our vision of what we want to achieve and our plan to take us there; somewhere along the way your community is going to disagree about the best route to take. After showing humility by listening and understanding, if we still believe our way is the way the community must go, we need to bring them around to our way of thinking. In fact, we must do more than that! For the plan to work and vision to be realised it is imperative they believe what we believe.

Social Proof

Have you ever been uncertain on what to do, which product to choose or how to behave? Have you ever found the answer by watching another person, who appears certain in their actions, and copying them exactly? It's the herd mentality from caveman times. We see a person or group doing something and believe it must the be safe or correct way to perform the activity as they are getting results.

Big companies use social proof all the time by having a celebrity endorse their product and appear on advertising material. They also use experts to vouch for their product; a great example is a dentist endorsing toothpaste. And then there's the less obvious forms of social proof such as buying a product because it has a lot of positive reviews, queuing for an ATM machine as there is a big crowd and purchasing a product based on what your friends say.

The key to making this work for your community is by convincing a few leaders to follow your idea. When the majority are uncertain on which idea to run with, they will look to the leaders for reassurance. If they see their leaders fully behind the idea, it's a no brainer, they will jump on board and never look back.

Contrast

If there are two things in sequence which are different, we will tend to view the second one as more different to the first than it actually is – this is the contrast principle. Here's a real-life example that you may have carried out at school. If you put your left hand in a bowl of cold water and your right hand in a bowl of hot water, leave them for a couple of minutes and then take them out and put both in a bowl of lukewarm water, the left feels hot and the right is cold!

Another example is when a car sales person shows us a few run down, overpriced vehicles before bringing our attention to a good condition, great value for money car. By contrast, the last one looks like a great deal and we want it more.

We can use the contrast principle in day to day life when we ask for something. Our natural reaction when asking for a favour or when we have a request is to reduce our ask. Let's say you want to borrow $20 from a friend. You will probably ask for $10 as it appears more likely to have your request accepted and then bump it up and ask for the whole $20. However, if you were to ask for $30 and then change your ask to $20 you are more likely to get a Yes to $20 using the second method as your friends feels they are saving $10, rather than lending you an extra $10.

Attack and Confess

This is something I learned from Tony Robbins, I've found it really useful and I know you will too! It is primarily used to overcome objections people may have to our products and services.

The first step is to attack the objections people give for not buying from you. This works best when you bring up the objections before your audience can.

Next, confess about being dumb in the past for letting the objections stop you, before you realised – insert painful outcome that keeping with this way of thinking led to - the aim is to make your audience realise the consequences if they continue to use this objection. You MUST confess and not attack who you are speaking with.

Let's say your organisation offers a time management course and the number one objection they give is not having enough time. When talking with your audience you would say something like this;

"One of the main reasons people don't go on time management courses is they don't have enough time! It's stupid right? I've been guilty of it in the past too and it was a never ending cycle for me. I told myself I didn't have enough time to go on these courses meaning my time management never improved and I continued not having enough time. The silly thing is; if you add up the amount of time I spent telling myself I didn't have the time, I could have used the time to go on the course! When I realised how silly my reason was I booked the course and the game changed for me. I have more time than I even realised, more time to spend with family, more time to create memories and more time to get the important jobs finished."

Likable

Who are you more likely to take direction from; someone you like or someone you don't really want to spend time with? If your community doesn't like you they are not going to listen to you.

Being liked is what network marketing companies are built on. If you're not familiar with the business model, I'll briefly explain it. Network marketing companies rely on word of mouth advertising – they do not have traditional advertising such as TV commercials and billboards. Distributors invite their friends and family into their home and pitch the products to them, making a profit on what they sell.

The attendees buy, not because they want the products or because the host is a particularly convincing sales person, but because they know or like them. Which goes to show we are most influenced by the people we like.

Robert Cialdini in his bestselling book – Influence states there are 5 main factors that cause the liking rule to take affect;

- **Physical Attractiveness** – we are more likely to think a person has talent, intelligence and honesty if we believe them to be good looking.

- **Similarity** – we like people who are similar to us.
- **Compliments** – as a rule we believe praise and like people who give it.
- **Contact and Cooperation** – the more we are around something or someone the more we like them.
- **Conditioning and Association** – we like products if our favourite celebrity likes it too.

Build Leaders

"A leader who produces other leaders multiplies their influences" – John. C. Maxwell

There are two types of leaders; one which attract followers and one who develops leaders. It is a very subtle difference however it creates a major difference in mindset and how they work. For instance, a leader who wants to be needed attracts followers, whereas a leader who wants to grow and develop leaders wants to be succeeded.

If you've worked with a leader who desires being needed it becomes apparent they want you to do a good job and work hard. What they don't want is for anybody being recognised as doing the work better than themselves. This also ties in to the fact that leaders who require you to need them will focus on your weaknesses.

Helping your followers succeed and develop into leaders increases your influence in the long term. All the leaders you create will build their own community, either within yours or outside, and those people will respect what you say simply because their leader, the one you invested hours in to build, will sing your praises. They wouldn't be where they are without you, this is what they will tell their team.

Decision

*"It is in your moments of decision that
your destiny is shaped" – Tony Robbins*

According to Roberts Wesleyan College, the average adult
makes 35,000 decisions every day! That's a lot, right?
These range from which cable channel to watch, to how
we like our coffee and what to wear. The overwhelming
aspect of this; as our responsibility increases so does the
choices we have and as a result the number of decisions
we must make.

What is more challenging is that our decisions affect more
and more people. As a follower, the decisions we make
rarely affect anyone other than ourselves and our inner
circle – close family and friends. Leaders have this turned
on its head; rarely do our decisions ONLY affect our inner
circle. The majority of decisions we make impact the
community, even if it is in a small way.

If leaders are unable to make decisions, they fail. Deciding
which way is best keeps the community moving and carries
on the momentum. When a decision takes too long to
reach the movement of the tribe slows just like keeping
the clutch down in car. The car will keep rolling and will
eventually stop, however it won't gain speed nor will it
reach its destination.

Be Certain, Not Right

Indecision comes from our desire to be right. We love being right, but more so, we love being told we are right. The feeling we get from being told we are correct, that there was no better way, that they couldn't have done it better themselves – justification. We want to be justified, it's more than a want it's an urge.

This is why we fear making decisions; what if our course of action is wrong, if our idea isn't the best one, if the whole community crumbles! This leads us to sit and ponder, to be uncertain. People will not follow an uncertain leader.

Take the car example; you are driving on the highway, there are three lanes and up ahead there is a red car which is changing lanes every time it comes to a junction. It moves over to the slip road and then at the last minute swerves back on the highway. This driver is unsure about where they are going. How does the red car make you feel? I suspect nervous and afraid they will cause an accident. Do you want to follow this car? No! Your immediate thoughts will be to get as far away so you and your passengers are safe.

The same is true of leadership. The tribe will not follow a leader who is unsure. They would rather you leave the highway at the wrong junction and be certain it is the correct one, than stay on the highway and be indecisive.

Solve indecision by focusing on being certain over being right. If your vision is clear and your WHY is strong you will reach your destination.

The Richard Branson Effect

Richard Branson: founder of the Virgin Group and not shy about making big decisions. Looking at what Richard has achieved throughout his business career you will be in one of two schools of thought. Either you believe he is incredibly lucky, or that he took huge risks to achieve his success. The truth is he uses a decision-making strategy to 'eliminate' his risk.

In fact, he was asked by a young reporter years ago how he could take such mammoth risks; his response – "when assessing any opportunity, I ask myself two very simple, but powerful questions:

1) What is the worst possible scenario that could occur if I move forward on this opportunity?
2) If the worst possible scenario happens, can I handle it?

If the answer to the second question is yes, then the decision is made and I move full steam ahead – and to me that removes the risk."

Emotion

Remove it. That's this section finished, let's move on. I'm kidding, there's more to it than that.

Using the 'Richard Branson Effect' we know what the worst-case scenario is and that we can handle it. Leaving us to focus on our goal – the ultimate outcome. All decisions we make must be based on our outcome and not on how we feel in that moment.

There may be times when a decision has to be made, the natural response may be to shoot from the hip and go with your feelings. This is likely to be a subconscious reaction to keep you away from danger/risk and keep you in a safe, familiar positon – well inside your zone of comfort.

When this happens take a moment, preferably alone, however listening to your thoughts with people around works too! Recognise the feelings that are stirring inside and aim to understand if they are just passing through or are they resonating because the decision affects your goal.

From this you can acknowledge the feelings, remove the emotion and make a decision with your head which takes you another step closer to realising the vision.

Fast Decisions

One of the most common motivational quotes you will find;

"Successful people make their decisions quickly and change their minds slowly. Failures make their decisions slowly and change their minds quickly."

Why is it that successful people can make decisions promptly? With the amount of information they receive and the responsibility they bear, surely it is reckless to make fast decisions. The answer is found, as it so often is, in a clearly defined WHY. Successful leaders, know where they're going, know where they are taking the tribe and when a decision springs up, they know what choice must be made. The decision may be wrong, however as long as they keep the momentum and keep moving, they will reach their goal.

Making fast decisions is like a muscle which needs exercising to keep it's strength. The more decisions we make, the better we get and the faster we reach the end game.

When all else fails and you need to make a quick decision that you don't know the answer to, ask yourself the following question and go with the first thing that pops into your mind – "I know you don't know the answer, but if you did know what would it be?"

Wrong Move

So, you made a bad decision. It was going to happen at some point. With the number of choices at your disposal and the ever changing, technological environment we find ourselves in, wrong moves are something we cannot avoid.

But, with the right mindset you can quickly turn a bad decision into a fantastic opportunity. Here's my 4 step strategy for doing exactly that;

- **Act quickly** – As a species we tend to spend 95% of our time dwelling on the problem and only 5% of our time on the solution. You've taken a wrong turn – big deal! Move it out of your mind and focus on getting back on track.

- **What's the remedy** – Now you are in the present, it's time to analyse the solutions and pick the one which you most believe in. Bring the problem to the community and see what feedback you receive.
- **The lesson** – Could the bad decision have been foreseen? In hindsight, it may be obvious that the idea was a bad one – what can you learn from it? And how can you ensure it doesn't happen again?
- **Share** – It's a lot easier to sweep the wrong move under the rug and keep it to yourself than it is to tell people about it. Here's why it's beneficial telling the world; 1) the more times you tell the story, the more you hear it and the more you can learn. 2) The more you tell the story, the more likely you are to help someone from making the same mistake.

Listening

Good leaders are smart enough to have great people around them, but great leaders ensure they listen to those people. And by listen, I mean actually hear, digest and understand what is being said.

Most people, and I've been guilty of this, listen with the intention of replying. With wowing everyone in the audible vicinity with their amazing reply. This is the opposite of what needs to happen. The single greatest factor to effective listening is; stop thinking about what you are going to say next and focus on what the person is saying in that very moment. If we are planning our response, we are not actively listening.

You may think people cannot tell you aren't giving them your full attention, but they can. Have you ever been talking with someone and notice them glance over your shoulder? It's annoying right! And makes you feel undervalued and not heard – this is a prime example of someone who is not actively listening.

In a world where there are more and more people screaming for our attention, give the person you are communicating with the gift of yours by listening to them.

Be Heard

People want to be certain you have heard what they said, they are less concerned whether you do what they said. If a member of the community shares an idea they want to be heard and more importantly they want to know you have heard them.

Here are some of the ways you can show you are listening;

Eye Contact – Giving the person who is talking eye contact shows your attention is on them. You're not distracted by your phone or the person next to you, the speaker is without doubt as to where your focus is.

Head Nodding/Smiling – Moving your head up and down sends approval signals and encourages the person to keep talking. Don't nod your head too much as you may appear overzealous! Smiling is another great way, not only does provide encouragement, it also makes you feel good.

Questions – By far the most effective thing we can do to show the speaker we are listening is asking questions. The key is not to interrupt, wait for a pause in dialogue and ask your question with curiosity and enthusiasm. There are no bad questions, don't worry about looking silly as long as the person hasn't already answered the question, your question will enhance your reputation as genuine listener.

Speak Last

In group discussions, it is tempting to jump right in sharing your ideas, you may even feel compelled to do most of the talking however, it is more beneficial to speak last. Giving every team member the chance to share their thoughts before giving yours prevent what they say being influenced by you. If you throw your ideas into the group first, some team members will change what they are about to say so that it complements your idea rather than giving their genuine perspective.

Not only do you get to hear the team's ideas it also builds their confidence. They need courage to speak up and put forth their thoughts to the group, who will pass judgement. No matter if the team like or dislike the idea, both build confidence.

After confidence comes the growth of leaders. Taking a back seat and hearing what others have to say allows their leadership skills to grow. Not only does creating leaders increase your influence (see the chapter on Influence) it also means you can focus on other tasks as those leaders will handle what comes up. The more activities the community can focus on, the more results will happen and more goals will be accomplished!

Can't Do It Alone

You are not going to have the best idea every time. There is no hiding from this, it has to be accepted for you to get the best not only from your team, but the whole community too!

Most of the great ideas are going to come from the tribe working together on the same goal. This is Napoleon Hill's

Mastermind Principle working in full effect! Two or more minds are better than one.

Ideas come from things that have inspired us, the more people involved in coming up with ideas the more moments of inspiration will have taken place collectively. To find a solution to a problem, overcome an obstacle or create the next game changing product; the moment of inspiration needed to do all those things may have been experienced by someone else. In order to fast track the idea generating process and the success of the community, work in groups rather than on your own.

The bouncing of ideas from one person to another and back again will take rough, part ideas and turn them into specific solutions. Having said this you may find the best ideas come when the discussion has ended and the group has had time to go over what was said.

Don't Interrupt

This is something I need to work on. The person I'm listening to will be talking, it could be about their day at work, what they did last week or an idea for the progression of the community, and I will have a question or an idea and being impatient for them to hear it compels me to interrupt.

This not only ruins the flow of the conversation, but it appears to the speaker as though I value what I am saying more than them. This is contradictory to what I mentioned in the previous section on the best ideas coming from the collective effort of the community.

If you too recognise this tendency in yourself hopefully the following points will work for you as they are for doing for me;

- **Write it down** – Most of the time I interrupt because I don't want to forget what I want to say. Rather than blurting it out, now I take out my pocket journal and write it down. This is easier to do when in a meeting and can invoke questions when it's a one on one conversation, but I would rather the person I'm listening to ask me questions than be interrupted!
- Lips shut – If I still find myself interrupting I focus on keeping my lips shut. I pay attention to my lips and keep them tightly sealed throughout the conversation.
- Practice – As with any new ritual, the only way for it to become second nature is by practice. I recognise I have interrupted, apologise and make I mental note on what I will do next time I get the interruption urge.

Body Language

Listening isn't just about using our ears, we need our eyes too. There is a well know statistic that only 7% of how we communicate is through our words, so what makes up the 93%? Well, 38% is how we say something and a whopping

55% is body language! That means over half of how we communicate comes from the way we move our body!

In order to fully understand the person speaking we must read the signals they give out with their body movements and posture. For instance, if you are in a one on one meeting with a colleague who is expressing a few concerns about working for the organisation and they finish speaking. Reading their body language, you may be able to sense that they are not really finished and push them for more.

After probing them, they may confide in you a deeper source of their unhappiness. Once you know their true problem then you can really help them rather than masking over it.

Reading and understanding body language takes time to learn, one of my favourite books on the subject is Body Language by James Borg – check it out!

Responsibility

Why does one person get chosen for a promotion while others, with equal experience, knowledge and skill get looked over? There are many valid answers to this question, I believe that a person's willingness to accept and behave responsibly is a major factor. In addition to being overlooked for a new role, responsibility can make the person selected turn it down, with the common reason "I don't want the responsibility".

Great leaders pass the credit and take the blame. If the organisation wins, the team is the star however, if it fails, it is the leader who must hold their hands up and say "this was down to me".

As a leader, you are responsible for a tremendous amount - setting the example, the welfare of your followers, the direction of your community, improving the community daily, focusing on the big picture, asking the tough questions, having at least a basic understanding of every role within the organisation and many more! It is understandable that the responsibilities of leadership can weigh heavy on a person's shoulders.

Handle The Pressure

There is no hiding from responsibility when you decide to lead. It's like success and failure, rain and clouds, Beyoncé and Jay Z, they come as a package deal. The people you lead will look to you for help, guidance and to know what you expect from them. This can be difficult to handle not only for new leaders, but for experienced leaders entering new teams.

One thing that is a huge help in relieving the pressure is early wins. Getting results within the first three months will build confidence in your followers that you are the right person for the role. You'll feel some of the pressure lift, you will relax and that's when you will perform at your best – when you're more concerned with the pressure you put on yourself to do your best than the pressure you think everybody around has placed on you.

Early wins don't need to be huge results, nor do they need to be quantitively measurable like an increase in profit, membership increasing or a decrease in complaints. They can be an idea that the whole team believes in and gets behind, something as simple as changing the layout of the office to be more productive or knowing everybody by name before you take the role.

Their Mistakes Are Yours

If the team makes a mistake, this is your responsibility. Bestselling author Napoleon Hill goes a step further by saying: "Successful leaders must be willing to assume responsibility for the mistakes and shortcomings of their followers. If they try to shift this responsibility, they will not remain the leader."

You may be wondering – why do we need to take responsibility for your follower's actions? You are the person they follow, the person who gives them direction, the person who will be held accountable if the vision isn't realised and you are also the person who will be put in the limelight for the world to admire if the vision is achieved.

If a member of your tribe makes an error it may be because your direction wasn't clear and as a result the person didn't understand what was being asked of them and the exact result you desired. Or you may not have listened to them. If the team member is carrying out a different role to you they are likely to have a greater insight into what will and won't improve the outcome.

Ultimately, if you believe what was being asked of them was clear, they have all the resources they need and you have listened plus valued their input, it may just be they are not cut out for the role. This is your responsibility. They are on your team, move them to another department or show them the door.

Strengths and Weaknesses

A leader of a group of people with the same purpose, who desire the same result, who have the same beliefs can be likened to the conductor of an orchestra. If you imagine every instrument in the orchestra represents the qualities of its player, the conductor becomes the person responsible for creating music by bringing different sounds together. If even one musician is out of time, playing too loud or playing the wrong note, the whole piece of music is ruined.

You have exactly the same responsibility leading your community. Every single member will have a different combination of strengths and weaknesses. One person may be exceptional at marketing and lousy at accounting, it is down to you to recognise what they are good at and put them in the most effective role. When they have taken the role, the next step is having them work on tasks they are great at. For instance, your new team player who has moved from accounting to marketing may be better at social media than updating the website, it becomes another challenge getting each team running to their optimum and beyond. Hopefully, you will have great management around you to help develop each department, as doing all this on your own will become too much as the organisation grows.

More Than Paid For

In Earl Nightingale's Strangest Secret, he states "One of the penalties of leadership is the necessity of willingness, upon the part of the leader, to do more than he requires of his followers".

It goes without saying that a leader of an organisation must give more in value than they expect from their followers. However, this is the opposite approach most people have towards their job. How often have you heard the phrase "that's not my job" banded around the office? I'm guessing it's quite frequent, possibly daily! I know I heard it too many times during my accounting career.

As a leader, these moments provide you with an enormous opportunity. When most around you are dispelling tasks with reason such as; "that's not in my job description" or "I don't get paid to do that" you can take on the task, give it your best effort and hopefully achieve a result. Along with your peers noticing the extra responsibility, so will management above you, leaders in other departments and those with less experience.

This attitude quickly sets the example for everyone you come into contact with, people will know what to expect from you and what you expect from them.

I Will Make This Happen

When all is said and done there is only one person responsible for achieving the ultimate result and making the vison a reality. That person is you! You can't run or hide, it will find you.

This is a thought to relish. I say this because, if for whatever reason, you don't achieve your goals and are reflecting on your life when you are too old to work, what would you rather be able to say;

1) The people around me held me back. It could be family, work colleagues, friends
Or

2) I gave it everything I had, but I just wasn't good
    enough.

The answer is easy. I choose 2) all day, every day, for the rest of my days. I want the responsibility of the hustle because I want to know if I'm good enough to change the world; rather than have the regret of people holding me back.

Communication

"The single biggest problem with communication is the illusion it has taken place" – George Bernard Shaw

Another pillar which is vital to the success on any leader. It's impossible to become a great leader without being a great communicator. From our earliest days in education we are taught about spelling, grammar, vocabulary, enunciation and so on. While it isn't my intention to discredit these skills, they are important to have, the real art of communication is more subtle – hiding in plain sight.

Being able to develop an alert awareness of what's going on around is what truly separates excellent communicators with those who just get by. Studying the world's top leaders, you will notice a pattern – they are all fantastic communicators. They talk about their ideas, vision and purpose in a way that touches people's emotions. Great leaders understand the need to inspire their audience if their idea is to take root and develop.

One thing exceptional communicators have in common is they are great listeners and great at reading people. They can sense the moods, attitudes, values and concerns of the people they are communicating with. Not only do they read all this, but they have the ability to quickly adapt their message to meet their ever-changing needs of the audience.

Simple

KISS – Keep It Simple Stupid! As the old saying goes, the simpler the better. Your communication must be clear and simple for it to be understood. If you're wondering why, an obvious benefit is it saves time. There's less confusion, resulting in less time invested in explaining what you mean and what you want.

It is much easier to be complex, there is great difficulty in keeping it simple. To narrow down what you want to communicate into as few words as possible without missing any detail is no easy task. It takes thought, understanding and a burning desire to be understood. Albert Einstein sums it up perfectly "If you can't explain it to a six year old you don't understand it yourself".

According to Albert, the first step in simple communication is understanding what we want, then we can tell our team, customers and the world. If we are undecided this will reflect in our communication and create confusion. It may not be as obvious in a small group however, as more people encounter your message cracks will appear and different interpretations will arise. Eventually, what you want will be diluted as it spreads throughout the group.

Empathy

Many people often confuse empathy with sympathy, but it is much more. Google defines sympathy as "feelings of pity and sorrow for someone else's misfortune", whereas empathy's definition is; "the ability to understand and share the feelings of another". Put in Average Joe terms, empathy is putting yourself in another's shoes so that you can experience the emotions they are going through, be that positive or negative.

A key to being a great leader is the ability to place other's needs above our own. Empathy aids us in understanding those around us which in turn, helps us get the best from them. Not only can we comfort the team when they are low, we can congratulate them when they are on a high.

We can become an empathetic leader with one question – "Is everything okay?" With those three words we can dive into the life of our colleague, lessen the load of their burdens, share their excitement and console them. We can check they are actually okay and show that we care.

You may believe this is not your role however, who do you think a person will work harder for? A leader who understands and helps or a leader who only cares about the result.

It's Not All About You

Humans like talking about ourselves. When we engage in conversations it's easy to start sentences with "I did this", "I've been there" or "It was great, I enjoyed it". We keep the focus primarily on me, me and me. I believe we do this, not because we don't care or are disinterested with the person we are speaking with, but because we know a lot about ourselves and it's something we have always done without thinking about it – it's become a habit.

We can use this knowledge to get people to like us in conversations. Why do we want people to like us? We buy, follow and join people we know, like and trust. All we need to do is stop talking about us and start asking about them.

First, we must recognise we are talking about ourselves. If we are using words such as "I, me or my", it's time to stop. Next, we must shift focus onto the person we are speaking with, it's all about them. My favourite way is by asking questions with the intention of learning something new. Imagine if we could learn at least one new skill, piece of information or gain a different perspective from everyone, how enriched would your life be?

Speak With Your Hands

Earlier in the book I talked about body language as an aid to listening and understanding the speaker, now let's discuss the opposite – communicating using hand movements.

Our hands are the most obvious body parts we can use when speaking and this becomes more apparent when we must speak in front of a large group. When talking with an individual or group have you ever wondered "What do I do with my hands?" Me too!

Carmine Gallo, author of Talk Like Ted says "Complex thinkers use complex gestures – it's impossible for them to keep their hands still". He goes on to say "gestures give the audience confidence in the speaker". If all we must do to give our audience confidence in us is move our hands, then it seems silly not to. It can be uncomfortable to start with, there is only one way for it to become second nature – practice.

If moving your hands becomes too much to think about, Robin Kermode – Author of Speak so your audience will listen, gives this piece of advice "hold them lightly together in front of your lower stomach while standing".

Salesperson

All leaders are salespeople. Here's why;

- Salespeople can't make you do anything; neither can leaders.
- Salespeople are selling a vision and ideas; so are leaders.
- Salespeople know they are in a relationship business; so do leaders.
- Salespeople are influencers and persuaders; so are leaders.

With this in mind, we must communicate like a salesperson. If we want our community to do something or we would like an individual to carry out a task we must sell it to them. Just like we must sell the whole community on our vision, every member must believe in the WHY.

The subtle art of persuasion is key to making all this happen. In fact, persuasive communication can achieve five things;

Stimulation – Persuasive communication reinforces, intensifies and prioritizes existing beliefs.

Convincing – Sometimes a message is supposed to convince the listeners of the rightness of a certain decision or course of action.

Call to Action – The aim here is to get the listeners to do a specific action, normally a change in behaviour is required.

Increase Consideration – Here communicators are looking to slightly change how their audience views a topic, mainly used when the audience are opposed to what you believe.

Alternative Perspectives – This is the next step after increase in consideration. Here the goal is to ensure the audience accepts what we are saying even if they do not agree.

Mentoring

"Tell me and I forget. Teach me and I remember. Involve me and I learn" –
Benjamin Franklin

Leaders share what they know and help less experienced team members, the status as a mentor comes as a by-product. One of my all time favourite quotes on mentoring comes from Jim Rohn; "If you share an idea with 10 different people, they get to hear it once and you get to hear it 10 times!"

Sharing with someone could transform them. It could be the right moment for them to change, to see an opportunity in a different light. But, there's more to sharing what you know than aiding the listener. The speaker, you, could also be transformed. Hearing the idea over and over again reinforces the messages into the subconscious mind. And just like the listener, you never know which time could be the right time for the message to click.

Jim also uses a brilliant analogy, comparing the mind to a glass of water. If a glass is full of water, can it hold any more? The answer is Yes – if you pour some out. If you want more, you must pour out what you have so you can receive more. However, unlike a glass, the mind can grow and become bigger meaning it can hold more 'water'.

Safety

Mentoring is a two-way street. For all people involved to get the maximum benefit both need to feel comfortable taking and giving constructive feedback. As the leader, it can be nerve racking giving feedback more so when it relates to a team member's performance you want improving. It's a little easier when it's praise you are serving, but even that can leave you flustered and embarrassed. There's no getting away from it, you have to do it and it will get easier with practice.

What's more important is how the mentee feels. They need to be open to receiving constructive feedback plus understand you are doing this to help them improve, grow and get them closer to achieving their goals. And for the mentoring relationship to be a two-way street you too, must be open to receiving feedback.

If the mentee feels they learn the most by watching, but you prefer them to be doing, they need to feel comfortable saying this. This is your responsibly to put them at ease and create an environment whereby sharing constructive feedback is a positive experience. One to look upon as an opportunity to improve.

Be a Coach

At times your team will find it more valuable if you behave as a coach rather than a mentor. The difference is minor; as a mentor you give constructive feedback and push them in the right direction, as a coach you refrain from commenting and only answer open ended questions. The major key to being a coach is allowing your team to fail. You may see the mistakes coming, be able to prevent it on numerous occasions, but you mustn't.

This is the art of coaching. Having the foresight to know what mistakes you can allow without hampering the community's progress, while letting them make the biggest errors so they fail hard and improve fast. This requires you to be non-judgemental about the person you are coaching and to sometimes take harsh comments when the person you are coaching doesn't agree with you allowing them to fail.

The aim of coaching is to support your team and bring out the best in them. For you to be the most effective coach you must know where you want to take the person you are coaching. What is the goal, the end result, the finish line? Have this clear in your mind when you are working with them.

Embrace Failure

As a leader you most likely already know that failure is vital to success, I would go as far to say that you can't have success without some degree of failure. And as Rocky Balboa says "It ain't about how hard ya hit...it's about how hard you can get hit and keep moving forward".

The lessons we learn from failure are invaluable however, our team may not understand this and it is our job to help them see failure in the same light as us. Viewing failure as a positive experience is the only way they will keep bouncing back from being 'knocked down'.

Having the mindset of 'what can I learn from failure' before it happens results in the maximum learning experience should failure strike. Your team will need less encouragement to 'get back up' and, they will be searching for all the value hidden in defeat.

They can also embrace failure which is not their own, including yours, other team members and leaders outside your community (past and present) such as - Steve Jobs being kicked out of Apple, J.K Rowling being rejected by publishers for Harry Potter and the Titanic sinking to name a few.

Ask

"Questions are the answer, if you want a different answer, ask a different question" – Tony Robins

This is true not only for the questions we ask of ourselves, but the questions we ask our team. If our goal is to get the best from the people around us then we must pay attention to the questions we ask. For instance, if a team member has made a mistake, maybe they filed documents in the wrong place or didn't get a signature from a customer collecting an order; it would be easy to jump in with "That's wrong! Why did you do that?". When instead we could lead with "What was your thinking behind doing that?". The first question isn't a bad question if asked in a non-aggressive tone however, the second question is likely to make you appear curious rather than angry even if your tone is not on point.

To get the best from your team you need to understand them, questions are a great way. Most of the time one question isn't enough, especially if the person you are in conversation with has a problem. In order to get to the real root of the problem it will take around four questions. Be curious, ask probing questions and understand Why!

Storytelling

Do you know what most of the bestselling self-help books have in common? I'm sure you've guessed it – they tell a story. Usually, they are fables – a story conveying morals and values. Don't believe me? Here's just a few; The Monk Who Sold His Ferrari – Robin Sharma, The Richest Man in Babylon – George. S. Clason, The Go-Giver – Bob Burg and John David Mann.

Storytelling is so effective as it touches our emotions making us relate and engage with the person speaking. We feel what the speaker is saying, resulting in us being empathetic and understanding.

There are three types of stories we can use; can you guess which is the most effective?

- Personal – our own account, something which has happened to you
- 3rd Party – somebody you know, maybe a friend or family member

- Famous – the story of a product, brand or person in the limelight.

Have you guessed? Personal stories are the most effective! They work for a number of reasons; one of them is we know them the best. The experience happened to us so we know the little details that may be lost when we tell 3rd party or famous stories. It's mainly down to how we feel when we tell the story, our audience will only feel what we feel, for them to be moved we have to be moved, for it to touch their emotions is must touch ours, for them to understand we must also understand.

Summary

"Leadership and learning are indispensable to each other" – John F. Kennedy

You made it, well done. The 12 Pillars have been examined and the rest is up to you. Reading about them won't improve your leadership skill, neither will journaling. Only action gets results. As the old saying goes; practice makes perfect.

It's unlikely you'll perform the pillars once and they become habits, the end. That's not how the story goes. To see a change you will need persistence, effort and patience. If your WHY is big enough, the desire you have to realise it will pull you through the testing times and into the light. Your leadership skills will grow – Remember if it was easy everybody would do it.

For change to happen pick three pillars you would like to improve, these may be strengths or weakness. Three works because it's simple, you pick too many and it's easy to forget what is needed to improve. It's vital you begin implementing the changes right away, not "I'll start tomorrow", start right now, where you stand.

When you have selected the three write;

- Why you have chosen that pillar
- How the changes are going to happen
- What you are going to do daily

<u>Pillars</u>

1)

Why –

How –

What –

2)

Why –

How –

What –

3)

Why –

How –

What –

Now you have all three – Begin! Don't hesitate just do!

AVERAGE JOE'S

Secrets to Personal Development

JOE HINCHLIFFE

FREE EBOOK – get the bestselling eBook – Average Joe's Secrets to Personal Development:

JoeHinchliffe.com

Connect With Joe

Thank you so much for taking the time to read this book. I'm excited for you to implement the rituals in your life.

If you have any questions of any kind feel free to contact me at http://joehinchliffe.com/contact-mebook-me/

You can follow me on Instagram: @joehinchliffe

And connect with me on Facebook: https://www.facebook.com/joehinchliffeuk

You can check out my blog at http://joehinchliffe.com/

I wish you all the best for your future.

Joe Hinchliffe

One Last Thing....

If you enjoyed this book or found it useful, I'd be very grateful if you'd post a short review on Amazon. Your support really does make a huge difference and I read all the reviews so I can make this book even better.

If you'd like to leave a review, then all you need to do is click the review link once you finish reading.

Thanks again for your support!

Copyright Page

Average Joe's Pillars of Leadership: Defining Characteristics of Leadership